tomorrow is the tugboat of today.

Alan John Stubbs

Published by The Onslaught Press
19A Corso Street, Dundee, DD2 1DR
on 31 October 2018

ISBN: 978-1-912111-97-8

The text is set in **Le Monde Livre** by Jean François Porchez,
the cover and front matter in Akira Kobayashi's **DIN Next**.

Printed & bound by Lightning Source

*for Emma, Rachel, and Rebecca,
with love.*

Cuttings of the light

Conversations

Content

Pause before the flare

The ability to spool

Cuttings of the light

Snow

her birth changed everything

to white, white covering
the patchwork of fields making a field of light
to be negotiated
with greater care than before

her letter came with the thaw
to tell of colour's returning—
the raw umber path sunk in on the way to the stile
across the new wall

the elegant lettering is all that remains of that year's fall

she was so small his small hands were oversized
and fumbled
with her vests and dresses
buttons and fasteners, and the house
she built was a funnelled drift of her things that slowly settled

when she left it was to live in warmer climes
in an easy fluid form, and to dance through the night

as lightly as when she was first airborne

there is something about seeing flowers in the rain

film shots of crowds and disguised by colourful umbrellas
the main characters make a clean getaway

Open the door? As if . . .

She carries demons in a case,
brings in fences,
and fields of wheat—sun ripe.

She sits, waits for some
change, or slackening in the winds
that tend them.

He brings cuttings
of the light—

revolutions

inside the house he finds that there are stones
she has laid out in different patterns

some in a line that ends in an arrow head
are the vertebrae of a creature slunk into the wall that disappears

while others piled up the largest at the base
are grey and rough being all edges

or shiny smooth are the bright colours of different irises
cold pulled from their sockets and set here on the ledge

or in the fireplace as if to see whatever—
some have climbed the stairs to cluster on the cistern

others abide in flower pots and are watered inconsistently
not all the stones are hers—some

were carried here in Dylan's
pockets to be disgorged examined and weighed separately

the solid properties of each teased out by careful rotation
are then accorded the ancient rite of laying out flat

on an open palm so that the sun looking down
might pass a judgement on them

or consult with them in some way there is no understanding of
he finds they move about the house

making arrangements he has no knowledge of
rising up in cairns to detail

the thought that each moment however small
is a step that changes everything

A gift?

Tomorrow is the tugboat of today.
I think I'll pack to go away.

A house martin outside the glass—
door hops about the grass
to find a likely spot
for more of what it had before.

Two blackbirds mob a magpie out
of the tree.
Quarrelling loudly
until it's free, and they
can choose to stay, and nest.

Magpie circles, so do they.
There will be no rest this day.
Flit flitting branch to fence post,
shed roof to hedge, their
play is work and work is play.

Robin in the apple tree
scouts the ground and scutts away.

Branches move, leaves fan the air.
Magpie returns and settles there.

Blackbird in the tree nearby
is like a badge with a yellow eye.

Blue sky turns to grey.
All can wait another day.

Then grey whites—
                    and a grey
squirrel ascends the bole
with ease flick flicking out
his brush-plume tail, as if to teach
                                    what?

The very light?
The balance of it?

the broken blades

scattered atop the damp new-cut grass are
small sadnesses
waiting to become attached
to the soles of whoever passes
on crossing the sloping bank of the raised
mound that was made to hold back
or at least delay, the rising waters

of a river that one day will take all

there was news of a death in the mail
and this, or the abruptness of it, its waiting, calls back
to what had been good

of the person

for it seems that is all that anyone
could want—to be taken

further on the way
by those following

the way that these leaves of grass are

We had barely met—
I would that I had known him better

Like an anchor

holds close to the shore
it used to be a wise sailor
would tend a crow,
keeping it close
on a long journey, so
that lost he might throw it
up out of the nest
to soar high above
the clouds and see
a line they could follow
to safe land

and tomorrow . . . . .

being and not

thought boarded the wrong train
bound for Glasgow Central
to call in at the Cafe Gandolfi
breakfast on something good and hot
porridge perhaps, and a green tea

it took a seat with grain and character
running all through it - sat
under the large window that is a sea
of leaded glass that
fish formed only of light can cross

they might turn toward us
dry creatures
enter our World
of unsupporting air
be heavier and lighter
and be drowned there

each one, lit from behind, shines
with barbed fins made of jewels
of flaming yellow, like fine citrines

hard to imagine there are gills
razor blades hidden beneath flaps of skin
working, filtering—

it is better to keep to the blue
one is used to
though there is something unbearable
about being separate—as they
are hanging still, a darker blue
in a vague blue surrounding

of sea—its cerulean sheen
the colour of snow at first light—cool
bright—the reflective glow
carries no heat

beyond is the city street of flat
fat faced buildings propped by scaffolding

I stand on the platform, waiting

Buyer beware.

this mind is a Belfast sink waiting a buyer
in a kind of cheap antiques and junk shop where
happiness alights on objects that are
all lost, or strays
the twin purposes of containment and release play
out in different ways
in an eccentric landscape—a locked geography
it wouldn't do to simply stand on the threshold of
consulting a map, or
looking in
with short arms and long pockets

time is a gold penny watch whose stilled
hands tremble
on the turn of a use-blunted screw

sound is a small tin box that once opened
to free a tattered bird who sang until
the small brass key at the back stopped turning
as it had relentlessly, over, and over

the future is a jar of wild Poppy seeds, and another
of poor man's Capers in brine precariously set
on a tilted shelf
that gravity ever nudges south

connecting all these there are scampering Woodlice
whose brittle
segmented shells are bodies that scratch
scrabbling in the valuable dust
that is a telling collection
of marks—rudimentary runes

and outside of all
is the heavy load of body

Conversations

the abandoned shoe

on the pavement is the kind of relic
often found on an early walk

the narrow toe has opened up into the blunt-twisted
smile suffering can make, and the inner sole,
forced out, lolls alongside of it like a tongue robbed
of its alphabet, whilst the leathery black housing
gleams, as if the former tenants waxing and polishing
only that minute stopped, and apart
from the obvious injuries suffered, it is

diminished by being alone, this
dumb shoe speaks of violent acts in being

where a hard frost silvers the grass
to crisped leaves, and the sharp hardnesses underfoot

make a small sadness of it, there unrighted

trees are busy growing birds

they catch and throw, stretching limbs
all sleeked with rain, till every join
does creak and groan in the half-light
creatures roam unseen

as the turning begins that will
green the columns of the hill
in the strengthening to come

they may be refugees, no home
remains they could return to—
as bodies do, their mouths
and noses full of soil

the dumb know interleaved tales

the spiralling conversations of growth

Dream

When I realised she was made of ash
and all of the talking, talking, talking. Not

the ash that consolidates about a sapling
but what remains after a fierce conflagration.
A black and grey ash that disperses
eventually breaking to a dust, rather than
the rich blood ash that burnt peat becomes.

When I realised she was made of ash
and waiting, waiting, waiting for some

words to stop her from breaking, I was
afraid that a touch would dry the river
or raise a flood, and understood that her
words would be a wind to raise the good
earth from the charred bones of the land.

the house that should be flowers.

having alighted on the doorstep
to wait as the light-lengthened for the door to open
it may have known that with the ragged heat as it was
there was little chance

it goes without saying that trembling
first thing there on the red painted step
its wings, as yellow as the summer light seemed
to hint at dance

often spiders would march right in
as if reclaiming what was always theirs
climb the stairs and disappear
to fold their scaffolding in some dark recess

the moth, a hesitant vibration, was fissile
material soaking in thermals on the threshold
was dry energy itself changing form
to bristle there in a futile rage

or perhaps, unrealised then, breaking grief

time was . . .

behind the cracked window of the eleventh hour
building a simulacrum of a bird

is standing alone in a room on the first floor

there is nothing there to disturb
the building, it has stood empty since the flood
took possession of the road, and

the river took whatever was good

This is not about the whale.

With spears and barbed hooks
they forced a starless black
state upon what was
a World itself

Kept it close as it bled
a foam halo of blood

Closed its mouth, and sewed
the lips shut
so that it can not
take on water

so that it will float to shore
and its dismemberment

This could have been
a fluid a whale might swim in
and sing, but a whale
sized absence from the beginning
affected the current, the dri..ft...

Water is lead without it...
in the absence of song

What is it holds so long
that there is no turning away?
The mute eye?
The trapped tongue?
a delicacy I understand—

There is no reply

on a good day he sees trees inside

the tiles he stands on while he washes
whatever there is of the night,
its absolute nothing, away
and dries to a light of certainty.

on a good day the skies clear, and

all the green busies itself increasing,
the dogs of war lie quiet as logs, and . . .
the particular crow that ascends the ridge
tiles of the roof, landing two footed

clumsy as a child hopping, cleans
its self, rubbing its beak one side, then the other,

at the highest point where it takes surveillance . . .

rail replacement bus service.

the green gleam of leaves turning
metal, fragile, brittle, is changing

as we traverse water that is still
across the road on the way in to Aspatria after

the flood, just a small flood this time
three hundred or so houses emptied out

Oh! but the light is breaking the sky
through a low cloud so forbidding

up high is a blue clear high, and the view
as we descend to the train station by

the Lake District Creamery with it's ageless
sign, a black and white cow and a milk churn—

is of a builders yard with a white van, and the usual
stacks of used wooden pallets

the bus reverses into to turn back
up the road at Johanna Terrace—but what

a light—all encompassing
everything bright as a button

a yellow wagon smiles into reverse letting us on
two horses in a field are waked by the sun

West Street Health Centre stands ablaze
while across the street the Red Lion slumbers in shade

the black faced sheep never looked so clean
electricity pylons are positively gleaming

and the tops of hedges shocked into a last
thrust up in the air

are a child's hair under the influence
of a Van de Graaff Generator

—amongst the fabric of

grasses, shrubs, and herbs, and the architectural
languages of trees, he feels that raw
energies releasing are transforming, so
that the scamper of the disturbed that then
halts, quivering,
as if tuned in to a pulse that is all
about, connects to a stream
that runs hot, and is running

each to others, a complex
of being, that pauses

as the cut raw of it sutures the

threads that left alone will dwell

a history

a bird
not particularly rare
not particularly interesting
in many ways like myself
is trapped inside the glass and polythene
structure inherited from the man
who worked this plot before

opening the door, I wedged it
apart with a rock

the bird beat against the glass

time and again, and working
elsewhere I found it left my mind

gladdened by its absence

when I went back in to clear away
the tangled web of reachings
sun and water had violently thrown up—

a rigging of thick stems and grappling iron
tendrils that hoisted aloft the broad sails
set out fair, that had conspired to make
four solid pear-green impenetrable gourds—

the stems and leaves had yellowed
to a withered rope that caught on
to the tangle of what was already decaying

the bird was gone, and I left the gourds
set on a tray inside the door

Call to stay.

black was full of rain
and now a slick grey
is breaking over the hills
making a green of fields
caught between barbed wire,
                    stone wall, and fence
as the land rises to a line of far distance
and grey skies pink dully
like a wire that has died being blown on softly
then light comes and red fades over

a scene I have seen many times, and never
                    once travelled

a place I seem to know and have no knowledge of
of damp grasslands that are pasture
boggy in places and sometimes set with reed
trampled by days heavy cattle who
feed as they wait for the call to the milking shed

there will be the usual rough cobbled farmhouses
with machinery that mustn't be touched
where barking dogs watch to make sure you stay
on the road, and close the gate
sliding the bolt all the way home

there will be dirty streams
where water articulates dreams of shiny green
moss and fern in a language
that changes so quickly that trees must stand
in line, and take a draught
bending towards it, and every living thing
about visits, stooping to listen,
and birds made dumb by distance—that were stitches
crossing the sky—roost here

along with every other creature

Beauty.

a burnt russet
moth singed the electric light
unable to resist

it returned to the burn then plummeted
down the wide neck
of a deep cream vase on the sill

 brim-full of the water that was
incessantly dripping from the faulty
tap they repeatedly failed to repair.

Sure it had drowned
he opened the door
and carried the vase outside

only to find it had climbed
out of the waters cool embrace, and
fixed to the side of the vase, momentarily

as if a flux

dismembered.

the cobwebs that were worn rags stretched
almost to breaking between the poles at the boundary
where underfoot the wooden planks give way to grass
and have disappeared, as if drowned in the growing light

no rain or dew weights the tentative silk
and the way on through appears clear
and it occurs that only those most reliant on sight
as their guide would ever be caught in such a trap

and I understand why they say a blindfold would help us to hear,
and that we are always humbled by who we are
yet when day calls on the starlings to gather and wheel
in patterns we name 'murmurations', this doesn't matter

Content

Happiness is

a stockpot of enough
good rich curry to make
two or three meals of

and a large iron pan
full of plums waiting to be boiled to jam
a book to read when the boiling's done

and more than this
someone who likes to share a kiss
and walk the aisle between the trees

others have walked, and talk of those
things that only they may think of
while on the river slowly flows

to bring us, as it does
everything along the way

rumour

had been white faced afore
gone to ground and come back
altered beyond any semblance

exhausted he sleeked out
of the slit trench, his birthing scar
reborn of the wet earth
limped away, his shoulder crazy
a wounded animal, or something not finished yet

see the way the blues were
hid inside of the soil coat he discarded
only visible when rain occurred
at a certain slant to the sky
the hues—all of the hues sorrows
running, such gritty scree
they must be buried

in the futtered gasp of day
his palms would carry coin
across bog fields where
the vagaries of failure skirt
the upstarts of the town

stone—stones weathering

are erosive
oh, the fricative grit, wearing—
the rub of it

there used to be a drum in his chest
beating shot through his wrists, and ankles

now there is a bird big as a baby's raging fist
on a low branch of the one tree
the wind-small'd gnarled tree
by the slit trench he—
a bird with a black capped head insistently
hammering at the branch, its beak
sounding each blow, its short tail

tipping it judders

rain in Madrid

wakes up and punches the clock
and does not punch the clock

just as the firs are not weeping
stoically waiting outside in line
as drips roundly beat time
on the two windows opposite

where a line thrown across
has clothes hanging from it
that get wetter and wetter

it patters the awning that shades
a potted cactus sat on a small table

as it falls it adopts
a perfect round all unknowing
or joins—crashing

a number of cherry trees severely
cut back—who's white
flowers gather at the ends of branches
whose petals clutter pot and pan balconies

tomorrow's sun will bring
cats mewing, and a shadow
bird that pecks on the other-side
of the canopy that shields us from the light

revolution 2

what he thinks of is not the food, though the food was fine
or the drink, though they drank lots of wine

what he thinks of is the talk, although he forgets the words
and of her laughing as she used to when they first

met and went out together, though not to anywhere like this
posh vegetarian restaurant nestled in the lakes

what he thinks of is her face as she wipes away the tears
of laughter from her eyes, and all of the years

somehow vanish, yet everything they've shared is there
for a moment when she tells him not to embarrass her

if

he made love to her
he would begin at her feet—they might be cold

easing her toes
to the palms of his hands where hot goes

and understand that deep
underground rivers flow to an origin of open

sea, where she might be
at swim—an uncharted territory

outside of language

out in the open

trees have no cover
to offer, if they both could, and would,
at this time of year

a shield from the downpour
to shelter under, and wait
for what must pass, to pass

watching those less fortunate
who must be wet
traverse through rods of slanting glass

would be less harsh than being caught
like this—friendless
if ever trees could be thought friends

who lend a hand in emergencies
keep the rain out of our eyes
and stand awhile alongside us

comradely, quietly, hear, and sympathise
as they bear what trials they must, waiting

on reflection

what he was saying
when he said he saw his dad
signalman, electric meter reader, pianist, raconteur
looking at him
every morning in the mirror
was something about how the years wear the skin
so thin
the bones of the person become apparent

and perhaps something of loss
missing him
that is unending

and then again perhaps he is preparing
us, his offspring, for what comes

saying that even alone we are not alone

Creation.

Sleeping on the lightshade had perfected
the trick of retracting his legs and feet, so
only the toes of his dead man's shoes showed.

Pink Floyd played the song he'd said
ran in the blood like death, or the ache
of an old wound. He was
too frail to hack away a hole
and string a line through the compacted ice

of this day. Clouds were heavy, kept

closing in. Sun quickened,
etched mountains in leaf mould
that turned. Set
footprints across the shoulders. Composed
a text of fire to extinguish all
of the materials it had spun and woven, so
that only the thistledown that remained floats
settles wheresoever it may.

Things happen when people do not belong.
The weighted light was strange.

Action.

On route to Santa Maria del Popolo she tells him
'this cup of Americano is a deconstructed woman,'

that her eyes, lips, legs, and hips are set inside
the glaze, and that on the inside of the cups lip
is the legend 'illy espresso Pedro

Almodovar.' A young man
with a rucksack scoops water from the running
spout of a fountain, so that it is a fall of drops
catching alight he steps out into—

face upturned. A pigeon blinks
both its lids eclipsing a perfect round.

juego de nonos la pidola

streams converge
beneath the surface
gathering dark, grounding stones
to an edge

he says 'there is
nothing to lose.' she turns
'but there is, you see.'

the leaves
give to orange and yellow seeds.

on the far shore
a white dog sniffs the air.

the cloud will break.
she waits.

In Plaza Ayementa

shell fired air explodes.

sound ricochets then
off of the exclusive hotels and government buildings
all about. The man in front
hoists his girl up to see. Everyone
shouts and cheers. We
are bemused at this raucousness. Later
is the sea front, a coffee bar
named 'Vivir Sin Dormir',
the soft warm air of night, and stars
reflected on a water that never quite arrives

A drift

Geese seen from a distance are
smooth stones
the long necks and pointed heads tucked in
to near white pale sides

a strange geological feature
of the shingle beach, are
sleeping.

Walked to be beside the flat grey
sea beyond the snub nosed lighthouse where
a little push of jetty was
Blue skies clouded over
Watched the petty squabblers, those familiars,

of Broughty Ferry at Easter
The only visitors
not wrapped up against the driving wind

Geese turning

is it because the river

runs open throated
beneath a triumphant sky

the scrubby border occupied
by a standing army of Himalayan
Balsam with shocking

pink and brilliant
white cap badges

while Sycamore and Beech
having no sight
of the earth beneath

have splayed out feet, rise
implore the skies—desist

unable to see the Sheila Fell landscapes.

Air dances the wings of Cherry leaves
so that green shakes about the white frowsy hair pinked in the midst
of upraised arms shaking like a child's upbraided for walking
out onto a busy street
though it is restrained by an iron cage fitted about it and into the concrete
paving slabs diminishing what might be subtle yearnings

She has a patch, rather a coarse plaster, at her throat where
a piercing with a kind of stone is set in the wound

painfully healing. Her hair
that was wound up in a soft grey woollen towel is let down
so that what were flowers split apart and spill
about the slender bole out to the border-edges of the paving

where wall break stones tumble the corner of my eye
caught by the sleek grey of a wild cat turning away

Cape Town

before we were made to fear
riding the 'illegal'
taxis that would patrol
the busy roads to the city, we trusted
the rusty vans with benches
whose doors were always open
someone leaning out to beckon custom

knife scars on his face and arms
who cheaply took us wherever we wanted

empty.

As the children slept on she looked for the ghost
driven by her blood to find the other
but there was no sign of it anywhere on the coast
and the high grey waves turned to covers
as if shielding her at another's bidding.

It was too cold for the swings.
On the bare little green before the sea proper
is an unravelled world trapped in an hour
where unswimming clouds appear to be pale roses.
There can be no other story than this

simple bud that never flowers.
There are no ghosts here.

A line drawn.

She had looked at him knowing
and he had known
with no word spoken.

She rests within
objects he happens upon
and the red rim

clouds his eye

She is unused to being this empty.

She knows she is losing
'pound by pound'.

Her fathers dying words
'look after her' sound.

'I am full' the mother says.
The gentle daughter strokes her hair.

Lives on light and air.

making 1

towel wrapped about the loose and wet
she draws back
the locks on the door
and cool air rushes
in a garden brighter
as barefoot she prowls her lair

hands alighting on this or that insignificance

making 2.

She said 'can I wear your gold shoes
your posh shoes, your dolly slippers?'

There is a path of worn teeth, and a
silver line out in the water, and
beyond the steel bridge on the other shore
stones like footprints lead away.

The Moon

is almost but not
a white brush stroke
on a clear blue pallet

a Moth

small, hoppy, erratic
would go for it
become lost to something

attractive beyond measure
the idea
greater than the idea

infinity drawn tight

Pause before the flare

After Anselm Kiefer's Secret Life of Plants.

there is a tower of tin
shacks like those South Africans live in
in the shanty towns. (how quaint
the name sounds—shanty!)
laid out on the full skirts of Cape Town.
each has corrugated sides like those
cardboard boxes children play with.
with two doors cut but no windows
to let light in. they are stacked
one on another in a column reaching
straight up, like a tower—but without
classical form that suggests power
or grace. (i am told that they
are made of concrete). there is
something rootless about it.
otherworldly even, as if mis-spaced
set-down in such a landscape
of what might be ancient trees and ferns.

the base is a jumble of discarded frames.

beyond are scratchings
of root and branch

where Old Crow shits and hops
to a higher place to peck at breaks
in the surface he is beside, and waits
alert to the moving
crossing shadow lines that sun and trees
make—different time zones on the path
hazarded. ivy rustles.
sun is a white streak
in the grey. trees are growing
black. birdsong—distant voices.

After Anselm Kiefer's Urd, Verdandi, Skuld (the Norns).

the way that grass
or something that might be taken as grass
rooted in crevices
opens the wear of days—

though, of course, these strands are frays
of leather—in cement that fixed in place
un-counted bricks—a series of archways
—a vault of sorts, so the grass falls
to almost touch the flames

of the fire set on bare slabs, is

—considering it might be a kind of flax or hair
that trails, like a message
scrawled in chalk in a foriegn language

through gravity to the heat of the flames,

though it fails to touch them—
to connect
to the energies of flowers sparking
and sputtering, without catching at the fuse
—the grasses,

is that dead space—

was ever a more dead space set
within a vaulted brick chamber?—this

is waiting for release.
The pause before the flare

consumes everything—the infernal machine
seen from inside.

grass growing, but against nature.

Requiem for the Elephant in the room.

clearances did not really set in
                till eighteen hundred
as far as I know, though since
                they've been a constant

a biologist 'Grinell' first argued the role of climactic thresholds
                'a type of border'
                are they soft, i see them as a soft focus
in constraining the geographic boundaries of many species

we are observation rich 'Camille Parmesan' says
                and for a long time have been

i like dispassionate words such as 'land use change,
nitrogen fertilisation, increased atmospheric CO2'
i see a series of cages
                opening and closing
i especially like 'twentieth century anthropogenic global warming
has already affected the earths biota'
i find it is too advanced, and picture
        a spiral shift, a turning screw, a gyre
        we are fast inside
        with just one way to go
        turning ratchet like

there is an outflowing
of coral reefs, penguins, polar bears,
perhaps the damselfly

business gurus say 'less is more'

Please consider our art project where
the names of all of the creatures
that will soon be extinct are gradually erased

from all of literature leaving empty space

stirring

balanced on one hip
he sleeps
in the palm of her hand

In the experiment

it was necessary
to cut away the
eyelid and repeatedly
drop a pipette
of a certain
weakly acidic solution
into the soft
tissues of
the eye

mimicking rain

some do, some don't

"At the start of the day
a woman came up to the counter, she
slapped her toast down and said
'this toast is a disgrace,' turned
and marched away. Why couldn't she
at least be civil? The toaster's not working well.
We have to use the panini machine—it
only warms them up. It's
just no good, but that's no reason
to take it out on staff who are doing
their best, who apologised, and made
some more. What's her problem anyway?

She gets to sit eat toast all day."

woman crying—

the public phone has
swallowed all of the money
she eagerly fed it
giving nothing
in return

people sheltered
beneath a canopy
waiting for their bus, ignore
her fuss
and voluble tears

she looks at us plaintively,
in distress and I
feel the desire
to gather her up
and comfort her

but she is a stranger
and immediately a clear
voice says
'who exactly is this feeling for?'

Street life

they fly
to the window ledges and parapets nearby
to bicker
over unwrapped greasy litter
a colony inshore

of ice-pick heads
the fanciest of waistcoat button eyes
a coldness held within their gaze
where equations play out each surmise
as butter beaks tear and rip
to prise the flesh from under skin

the queue for the taxis thins
the waiter who came here one summer, and stopped
stops

lights go off, and doors are locked

When last I walked with her

the footpath along the river was
studded with felled and rotting trees
damaged by the flood

brown caps and a yellow kind of shelf
conjured fruiting spore—
bodies of wood they had mouthlessly

gnawed at as the sea
gnaws the shore
and she—sleeplessness
resting in her bones
who subtle as a willow bends
in the hollowing wind while the river
runs west to the sunset where

it finds a place
the half wild rooted
beneath her skin
willed itself into being

moves in water land and air
in the tocks of green woodpeckers
weaves tangles in her hair

Autumn Afternoon.

there are still flowers
by the wooden chair
with the carved letters—
'love me tender . .'
though the Sunflowers
fixed to a grill
against the wall, are turned
to heavy brown seed-heads—
unseeing,
though no doubt swelling
on the late thermals,
as they wait on avian
aided transition
to another place, another time.

The Cathedral bell rings,
though by my telling
it is twelve twenty three.
And a bird on a chimney—
trilling nearby, competes. A Bee
heavily bumbles grasses
by the Lavender. It seems
thrilled. Everything is pleasure.
A couple passing, hand in hand,
read 'how to live with Arts and Crafts'.
It is difficult to understand
the madness of the iron gates.
What is the point of these when
crossing the bridge at night I know
foliage will be grey cloud in a black

rushing sound of water weighing

The ability to spool

Cross here

where the tarmac is caked over foot-worn
wagon-worn cobbles where
the brick abatements of terraced houses stand
back retreating into shadow, and the
rainwashed drains sputter down cracked
dark leakings to the black iron palings that
hold strange others at bay, cross here
hobble quickly away, solitary, aware
as the disguised cobble edges
bend the floors of your shoes

Lettuce

the music of the soil
            in my mouth is
a watery sun
            of cloudless skies
                        leaves wet and crisp
                                    intensify
a limpid kiss that would
                        be a beard of moss
                                    or frets of a growling
repertoire
            whose verbal cud carries all of the weathers
                                    of a certain space
between careful footfalls
                        within a cage
                                    where a plain terrace is
where all beasts are discouraged
                        and fruit trees breathe out
                                    notes of green wood
and soft fruit resonate
                        concentrating idly in the light
                                    mimicry of the same wind
that splits damsons sadly to the ground
                        to be absorbed as they dry out
                                    like wetted cloths
                        across all of the gardens in a line
            on those washing days that burnt
a landscape strange
                        that unfurled
                        still is unfurling

household gods

she, a sofa curl
warms under idling hands.

the charred woman on the mantle looks
to the wall. the family
photographs stare.
                    the polished
stinkwood man of Africa
walks into space
his swollen belly, his rigid stick,
and pointed beard speak.

the ships clock ticks.

and the solid black god, his eyes closed, mouth open,
prays, as the crook dangles off his arm

In the city

spring trees
even this one
standing alone
are a flame
unreachable

veins burn to embers
each scorch is consumed
songs of blossom
moving through them
catching at the boughs

even in sleep they burn
restless hung with lanterns
innocent moment to last
moment as fire
outs old clothes

leaf follows leaf

She asked for the dead

wood at the gate
for kindling to save
the gathering

a scaffold dismantled
will bud other limbs
choose a space to bathe

heat opens
flowers from a prison
of the suns burning

all definition
working itself to a turn
of light escaping, speaks

swim she says

out of the cold salt water
hair was inexplicably boiled sugar
lips a shell

eyes pearls closing, and standing
against the tide
gulls cry, and the sand holds

toes are anchors
no, there is no reason he remains dry
on the shore

a usual companion

of wind deshabilled black
walks through the park
sits where he sat
eats what he discards
watches slyly
sideways

to stutter to its feet
to be alone

scaffolds

we placed planking in trees
where the branching of the trunk allowed
like arguments it was as sound

we looked out through the leaves
days passed and we stopped climbing
to where the wind could share
to be all hidden in tree-cloaks
where thoughts were too big to be held

the nearest thing to flying
though we never left the nest of branches
seeing from this high the birds deserted
barbed wire fences around the playground

and fields where the cows are patiently
chewing things over, and waiting

tangles.

rain yesterday rain today
every green thing has a coat of shine

purple crowned chives are laid out flat
as if someone sat on them in the night

air having a cloak of weight depends, and only
the thick leafed and wooded stem stand

all others bow low
while the yellow nylon washing line stretches

pole to pole eagerly catching white pearls of light
to a string that runs the exact length of the lawn
orange flowers are damp Belisha beacons flaming
warnings at the paths untrammelled cross ways

long grown overgrown, as difficult a terrain as
the runways of the mind might be outside of any rule

there is something about
the ability to spool out in any and all directions . . .

and death will not age us.

the light that lights the fissures in the ice where
water collected and froze overnight
gleams a dull kind of white that is not at all white
like the black of absence at night
it might be solid blue when stars illuminate

this ice though does not speak the opaque
languages
of distance, or horizons, porous with possibilities
it is not eloquent the way that white often is
and such a force forced it down flat that
it thinned to a brittle blackened sharp at edges

made mute in a state of stilled oscillation
as if a universe were pressured down, and time
itself ceased, so that in a way it is like a fold
where sheep are held, and the white of their
lived in dirty-pelts is held in the nature of it

there is also the waxiness of a much used fat candle
whose molten pour has set in a lethargy
globularly shaped by the ending of energies
capacity to move, and the hint of rancidity calls
a pale block of butter on a china dish set beside

a coal fire, warming for the white sliced
Alice would always serve with tea

Winter's Spring.

—a decay of leaves, last seasons
energies wash of the trees
to dry matter, clotting underfoot
in this freeze. Fricative
material. I think of
the fullness of grass
sweet at the round plucked base
above the root we mustn't eat.
The blades all edges, thin
sails, wind mills turning
to seed the air without toil—

such folly to work against it all.

when we are separate

though we are never separated by more
than water or air
we are still held together
by conjoining days and nights resolving
into these three offshoots that also are

we are rarely alone, almost never
and when we are it is as if the other exists somewhere just out of reach
beyond a door that will open any moment
or a wall breached simply by thought

so that you are standing before me washing that blue and white plate
you say is important to you, though why?
that I had used for the strawberries I picked
hunting under the veil of leaves and around the spiky edges
in the heat where
the earth is dry
too dry, seemingly, for gifts such as these

Acknowledgements.

'Trees are busy growing birds' and 'The house that should be flowers' have been published in *SpeakEasy Magazine*, issue no 2.

'rail replacement bus service' and 'unable to see the Shiela Fell landscapes' have been published in the Handstand Press anthology *This Place I Know*.

The poem 'when we are separate' is displayed on the poetry board at Cakes and Ale cafe at Bookends, Carlisle.

Other Onslaught poetry titles

Poems for the NHS (2018) ed. Matt Barnard

Glengower (2018) Gabriel Rosenstock

Poems for Grenfell Tower (2018) ed. Rip Bulkeley

Anatomy of a Whale (2018) Matt Barnard

Mandible (2018) Ingrid Casey

Flower Press (2018) Alice Kinsella

Long Days of Rain (2017) Janak Sapkota

Orpheus in the Underpass (2017) Ross McKessock Gordon & Gabriel Rosenstock

ident (2016) Alan John Stubbs

the lightbulb has stigmata (2016) Helen Fletcher

Out of the Wilderness (2016) by Cathal Ó Searcaigh
with an introduction and translations by Gabriel Rosenstock

You Found a Beating Heart (2016) Nisha Bhakoo

I Wanna Make Jazz to You (2016) Moe Seager

Tea wi the Abbot (2016) Scots haiku by John McDonald
with transcreations in Irish by Gabriel Rosenstock

Judgement Day (2016) Gabriel Rosenstock

We Want Everything (2016) Moe Seager

to kingdom come (2016) ed. Rethabile Masilo

The Lost Box of Eyes (2016) Alan John Stubbs

Antlered Stag of Dawn (2015) Gabriel Rosenstock,
with translations by Mariko Sumikura & John McDonald

behind the yew hedge (2015) Mathew Staunton & Gabriel Rosenstock

Bumper Cars (2015) Athol Williams

Waslap (2015) Rethabile Masilo

Aistear Anama (2014) Tadhg Ó Caoinleáin

for the children of Gaza (2014) Mathew Staunton & Rethabile Masilo (eds.)